POWER SURGE FOR TODAY VOL. 2

30 DAY DEVOTIONAL FOR CHRISTIAN WOMEN
TO LIVE A HEALTHY LIFE FILLED WITH PURPOSE

POWER SURGE FOR TODAY

RUTH VERBREE

REEVERB PUBLISHING

Copyright © 2024 by ReeVerb Holdings Inc.

All rights reserved.

No part of this book may be reproduced in any form or by any electronic or mechanical means, including information storage and retrieval systems, without written permission from the author, except for the use of brief quotations in a book review.

ISBN: 978-1-989100-19-6

PREFACE

Dear Woman Chosen For Greatness,

To get the most out of this devotional, I recommend that in addition to reading on devotional per day, you also spend some time in prayer and reflection and write down your thoughts.

This 30 day devotional is made exactly for where you are in your journey.

I love you and am praying for you!

Without further ado, here is your POWER SURGE OF THE DAY!

Ruth Verbree

CHAPTER ONE

DAY 1 - POWER SURGE FOR TODAY

KNOWING THE GOOD SHEPHERD!

"I am the good shepherd. The good shepherd lays down his life for the sheep."

John 10:1 NIV

There are many shepherds out in the world today who we believe are good. There are many leaders on television, on radio, on social media and in the churches, but the Bible says Jesus is the GOOD shepherd. The Good Shepherd is set apart from all the rest.

The good shepherd knows us. He knows our struggles, our wants, our hurts, our needs and He knows our journey like no other shepherd does. We can take real comfort in knowing that The Good Shepherd understands what we are going through right now, this minute.

Your pastor, who may also be your shepherd, will never know you intimately the way the GOOD Shepherd does. No matter how hard he tries to get to know you, he will never know your heart. You may have shared some intimate things with him, but I'm sure he doesn't know the intimate details like the Good Shepherd does. The Good Shepherd will always supersede.

The Good Shepherd even knows our deepest secrets, the ones we have hidden and buried deep in our soul. In fact, the Good Shepherd knows us better than we even know ourselves. We don't have to ever hide behind a mask with the Good Shepherd; He knows when our smiles are real or when they are fake. He sees when our tears fall, or whether we are holding them back for fear of being seen. He knows our wildest dreams and He wants to give us the desires of our heart.

What a comfort it is to know that we have a shepherd who is watching out for us day and night. We are never alone and we never have to pretend because this shepherd knows our hearts. He knows our thoughts even before they are on our lips, and because of this, we can talk to Him about every problem we encounter and every joy we experience.

What will you talk to the Good Shepherd about today? Will you share your joy, your sorrow or your burdens with Him? Share from your heart because He cares, and He's waiting for you to share your life journey together with Him. Spend time getting to know Your GOOD Shepherd today.

Something to ponder:

1. How does the image of Jesus as the good shepherd, willing to lay down His life for the sheep, deepen your understanding of His love and sacrificial nature? How can this reflection inspire you to draw closer to Him and entrust your life to His care?

2. Reflect on moments in your life when you experienced the guidance and protection of Jesus as your good shepherd. How can these past experiences of His faithfulness motivate you to follow Him wholeheartedly and seek His leadership in every aspect of your life?

CHAPTER TWO

DAY 2 - POWER SURGE FOR TODAY

GOD'S UNFAILING AVAILABILITY!

"I call out to the Lord, and he answers me from his holy mountain."
Psalms 3:4 NIV

Did you call out to God today? God is always waiting for us to invite him into our life.

There are so many lonely people waiting for an invitation, waiting to be called, waiting for an opportunity, waiting for the right time, waiting for God to answer, but God is also waiting for us to call on Him. He wants us to open our door and He will come in. He desires for us to get to know Him better.

. . .

I know that many people are very lonely in their own little world, and it feels like over the last few years people have distanced themselves even more from getting together with other believers. When was the last time you met someone new? When was the last time you called someone to invite them over for a cup of tea? When was the last time you called on God?

I phoned a friend the other day and no one answered. It went directly to voicemail. I left a message, but did not receive a response. Days went by, and still no reply.

We can call on the Lord anytime, anyplace and from anywhere and He will always answer. He answers from His Holy Mountain. That, dear friend, is so amazing! He is never too tired to talk to us. He is never too busy to put us off. He is never going to give an excuse why He can't visit us because He will never let us down.

God is not going to disappoint us. He will never send us directly to voicemail because we have 24-hour service with God. He is there for us 24/7, and for that we need to be truly grateful.

We can call on God right now and invite Him along into our journey of life today. If we are struggling with personal challenges, let's give our burdens to Him. If we are struggling with weight loss, let's invite Him to the table and surrender our weight loss journey to Him. If we are struggling with loneliness, let's surrender our loneliness to Him and ask Him to be our best friend. If we are struggling with confidence, let's surrender our self-confidence to Him. If we are struggling with anxiety, let's surrender our anxious thoughts to Him.

Let's call out to the Lord and ask Him to help us with our struggles in this season of our lives. It's such a blessing to know He's always there with us, in the good times and in the hardships and the temptations of our journey.

Call out to the Lord because He is going to answer you from His Holy Mountain today!

Something to ponder:

1. Reflect on your recent interactions with others. Have you reached out to someone who might be lonely or in need of companionship? How might you extend an invitation or offer support to someone waiting for connection?

. . .

2. In moments of struggle or challenge, do you turn to God for guidance, support, and companionship? How can you actively invite God into your daily life and surrender your worries or difficulties to Him for guidance and comfort?

CHAPTER THREE

DAY 3 - POWER SURGE FOR TODAY

GOD'S TAILORED BLUEPRINT!

"For I know the plans I have for you," declares the Lord, "plans to prosper you and not to harm you, plans to give you hope and a future."

Jeremiah 29:11 NIV

This is definitely one of my favorite verses! It's a favorite for so many believers as it gives such glorious hope for our life journey.

The education system has IEPs, which are individual education plans for students. These plans are to benefit the students, not to harm them, but to help them prosper in their education. But God has an even better plan for each of us. I call it God's IGP (individual growth plan) for each one of us, and His plan is to prosper us and to give us hope and a future.

This IGP is a specific plan for you. God takes your gifts and talents and creates your own blueprint for living so that you have the skills to be prosperous in your life and you have a plan to live out your purpose with great hope for the future. We don't want to alter or make modifications to God's blueprint because we can't come up with a better plan ourselves; we can't make modifications that will be better than God's blueprint for our journey.

So why do we think our way is better than God's way? Why do we seem to think we can make even slight adjustments to the blueprint?

If you have ever had a house built, you know about the blueprints and making modifications.

So many times, modifications are done to suit our individual needs. I know when we built our own custom house years ago, we made about 5 modifications to our blueprint and they had to be reworked to suit our needs.

. . .

But with God's plan, there are no adjustments needed. He has the best plan for us that we could ever imagine, so let's stop trying to change His plan for our life.

God wants to prosper you. He wants to bless you. He wants you to live out your purpose and give you the desires of your heart. He does not want to harm you, but if you try to alter His plan, you could get hurt.

Let's claim this verse and stick to God's IGP for our lives. As we grow and develop in the knowledge and will of our Lord, we will prosper and have His hope for the future. What a wonderful gift this is to us.

No matter what your individual circumstances are, His plan for you is tailored to suit you. If your individual growth plan is for you to keep working on renewing your mind or to keep fueling your body like a temple, or to grow in your gifts and abilities to keep living out your purpose, God wants to prosper you.

Will you trust in His individual growth plan (IGP) for your life today?

Something to ponder:

. . .

1. Reflect on a time when you resisted following a path that seemed divinely laid out for you. What prompted this resistance, and what did you learn from that experience about trusting in God's plan versus your own desires?

2. In what areas of your life do you find yourself trying to modify or alter the course of God's plan? How might embracing His individual growth plan, without seeking adjustments, lead to greater fulfillment and purpose in your life?

CHAPTER FOUR

DAY 4 - POWER SURGE FOR TODAY

TRUSTING OUR DELIVERER!

"The Lord is my rock, my fortress and my deliverer; my God is my rock, in whom I take refuge, my shield and the horn of my salvation, my stronghold."

Psalm 18:2 NIV

We can rest and breathe easily knowing that we have a deliverer! He will deliver us from the struggles and troubles we have on our journey. I love that God is doing a work in our lives. He is our rock and our foundation and we can place our total trust in Him, our stronghold!

What is a Deliverer? We think of a deliverer as someone who takes something or someone and hands it over to someone else, as in delivering a package. We deliver presents to other people, and we may have had food or gifts delivered to our door. We have had Amazon packages delivered to our homes and we have probably all had flowers delivered to us at some point in our lives.

We have also most likely dropped off and delivered children into the care of a sitter or to the care of a teacher at school. My husband worked in law enforcement and many times he had to hand over or deliver a prisoner from his care into the care of someone else. There are many kinds of deliverers.

But...The Lord is our individual Deliverer! He certainly doesn't hand us over to someone else, like a package - No! This is a special deliverer. The Lord sets us free. He is our deliverer from the enemy. He has rescued us and delivered us from sin and eternal separation from God.

How does the Lord deliver us? He liberates us and sets us free through His death on the cross. He delivers us from our troubles, and from the penalty of sin and our own death. He delivers us and helps us in our time of need.

We can think of many stories in the Bible where God delivered his chosen people. He delivered Noah and his family from the flood. He delivered Daniel from the Lion's Den. He delivered Mary Magdalene from the demons. He delivered the Israelites when crossing the red sea. He delivered Jonah from the whale.

What has God delivered you from? Here is a list of things you may have been delivered from:

- I have been delivered from an obsession with food.
- I have been delivered from lustful thoughts.
- I have been delivered from jealousy over my friends who have more than I do.
- I have been delivered from an abusive situation.
- I have been delivered from an addiction.
- I have been delivered from tormenting nightmares.
- I have been delivered from pain.
- I have been delivered from bitterness from the past.
- I have been delivered from a spirit of fear.
- I have been delivered from the hand of the enemy.

Praise God that He is our deliverer in ALL our times of need. The Lord has come to save us, to rescue us and set us free from bondage. The enemy no longer has any power over us because we have been delivered! We can trust God to be our refuge and shield. We are safe in his stronghold!

Let's praise God for who He is and that He is our Special Deliverer!

Something to ponder:

1. Reflect on a significant moment or period in your life when you felt delivered or rescued from a challenging situation. How did this experience shape your faith or understanding of God as your personal Deliverer?

2. Consider areas in your life where you still seek deliverance or freedom. What steps or practices could you incorporate into your life to further rely on God as your Deliverer and find strength in His refuge during times of difficulty or struggle?

CHAPTER FIVE

DAY 5 - POWER SURGE FOR TODAY

DISCOVERING GOD'S RICHES!

"Whoever pursues righteousness and love finds life, prosperity and honor."

Proverbs 21:21 NIV

What an encouraging Proverb! This verse tells us how to find what we are looking for! So many people today are trying to find themselves and are in the pursuit of happiness or wealth or fame, but what they are really looking for and searching for only comes with pursuing Jesus, which brings a fulfilling, meaningful life with prosperity and honor.

This verse tells us how to find what we are looking for! To pursue means to seek or to chase after, so when we pursue righteousness and love, we will find life, prosperity and honor. And, it's not limited to only a few people, it says whoever pursues this will find life! That means you and I.

Righteousness is a big word that many of us don't really understand. It refers to the quality of being morally right and just, to live in an upright manner that reflects our walk with Jesus.

To love refers to the act of caring for and supporting others, also reflecting our walk with Jesus. Together, these values can help us find not only life, but prosperity and honor as well. These are all very positive outcomes from the pursuit of righteousness and love.

Why do we find it so hard to pursue righteousness and love? It seems fairly straightforward, yet we flounder. So many people are in the pursuit of happiness; we hear about it in the movies and we read about it in magazines. Yet the pursuit of happiness is so different from pursuing righteousness and love.

Pursuing righteousness is striving to be morally upright and just in one's actions and behavior, and this will mean making some hard choices that may not be popular, but they will be in alignment with God's word. This includes making decisions based on what is right rather than what is easy or convenient. It's so easy to take the wide road, but we need to remember that pursuing the narrow road is the way to life.

Pursuing righteousness can also involve taking action to correct past wrongs, and this can also be very difficult. It takes courage to humble ourselves and seek forgiveness, but this is love and it will lead to life!

Pursuing love can mean helping those in need, being honest and truthful, and treating others with kindness and respect. It may mean stepping out of our comfort level and loving the less fortunate people around us. Pursuing love may also involve personal reflection and self-improvement, as we strive to be the best version of ourselves and to live in harmony and alignment with God's word and His values.

Let's decide to pursue righteousness and love today and see how God changes our life. What an exciting way to start our day, in a new pursuit.

Something to ponder:

1. Reflect on a recent situation where you found it challenging to prioritize righteousness or love over convenience or personal gain. What could you do differently in similar circumstances to align your

actions more closely with pursuing righteousness and love?

2. Consider your current pursuits in life—career, relationships, personal goals. How might consciously incorporating the pursuit of righteousness and love into these areas impact your sense of fulfillment, prosperity, and honor in the long term?

CHAPTER SIX

DAY 6 - POWER SURGE FOR TODAY

STEPPING OUT!

"You will go out in joy and be led forth in peace; the mountains and the hills will burst into song before you."

Isaiah 55:12a NIV

When was the last time you stepped out of your house with joy, being led forth in peace?

My hubby and I just recently purchased a new vehicle from an automobile dealership and I can tell you that my husband definitely stepped out with joy! In that moment, stepping out with the keys to our new vehicle was a moment for me to remember. He had a big smile from ear to ear; joy and peace was written all over his face. He no longer had to worry about the old car not having enough power or about breaking down on the side of the road. This gave us a real sense of peace with our new purchase.

A new purchase may give us joy or happiness for a few moments, but this is not the kind of joy and peace that this verse is talking about. The joy and peace from the Lord is lasting and will be with us throughout our whole life journey, not just a few hours or days. The peace and joy from the Lord is indescribable. It is a joy that fills our hearts even when we are facing difficult circumstances and trials in our lives. It gives us a peace that surpasses all understanding.

When we have complete faith and trust in God, then we can step out totally believing that God will lead us forth in peace. Joy and peace are just two fruits of the spirit that we want to develop in our lives and as we abide in Christ and allow the Holy Spirit to work in us, we will develop the fruits of the spirit through our actions. But...it doesn't necessarily happen overnight.

This reminds me of the quote: "We don't plant the seed and eat the fruit on the same day!" The fruits of the spirit need to be developed and it takes time for the seed to grow and produce the fruit. What we can do today is to start taking action steps that will harvest the fruit in due time.

One way to step out with joy and be led forth in peace is to focus on God's promises. The Bible is full of promises that give us hope and encouragement, but we need to claim them. These promises need to be at the forefront of our minds so that we have peace even in the midst of difficult circumstances, where we still experience joy and the mountains and hills still burst into song before us.

When we practice gratitude and take time to thank God for all that He has done for us and all that He is doing in our lives, then we can shift our focus from our problems to His provision. This enables us to go out with joy and be led forth in peace.

Let's step out with joy and be led forth in peace today in whatever journey we are on. Whether we are struggling with relationships or struggling to lose weight, whether we are struggling with pain or struggling to move our business forward, let's be confident that God is with us and that He will lead us in the way that we should go.

With our confident faith, we can trust and step out with joy and peace today.

· · ·

Something to ponder:

1. Reflect on a recent challenging circumstance where you found it hard to maintain joy and peace. What steps could you take to focus more on God's promises and shift your perspective toward gratitude, even in the midst of difficulty?

2. Consider a time when you felt a deep sense of joy and peace in your life journey. What elements or practices were present during that time that contributed to your ability to step out with joy and be led forth in peace? How can you incorporate those elements into your daily life to foster a consistent sense of joy and peace?

CHAPTER SEVEN

DAY 7 - POWER SURGE FOR TODAY

DIVINE PLANS!

"Many are the plans in a person's heart, but it is the Lord's purpose that prevails."

Proverbs 19:2 NIV

How many plans do you have in your mind to do today?

Do you plan to:

- clean your house
- try a new recipe
- run some errands
- pay some bills
- shop for a new outfit

- meet a friend for coffee
- go to the gym
- get outside for a walk
- take care of your pet
- phone one of your kids
- talk to a neighbor
- write a note to a friend
- buy flowers for someone
- visit a sick friend in hospital
- volunteer at the church
- practice a new song
- do some exercise
- go to the bank
- eat healthy and stick to your weight-loss plan
- plan a holiday
- babysit the grandchildren
- go to a party

Wow! We have so many plans in our hearts and minds. Plus we have bigger plans for our future like getting married, having children, getting a promotion, owning our own business, planning for financial wealth in retirement and plans to travel in the future. But... God may have a completely different set of plans for our life than what we do. The Lord's purpose prevails, not necessarily own plans.

God is taking us through so much more in this journey than what we could have ever imagined. We have big plans, but suddenly a door closes. We don't get that promotion we were counting on or we find ourselves struggling with relationships and life doesn't go the way we planned. We question God and wonder why things aren't going our way; we just cannot understand. Our retirement doesn't look like it was supposed to and we find ourselves asking God... what are the plans you have for me?

We are not always going to understand, but we do know that God's ways are always higher than our ways and His thoughts are always higher than our thoughts.God is sovereign and we can trust that God's way is not to harm us, but to prosper us.

When we pray for God to use us and we want to do the will of the Father, then we must trust that when He shuts one door, another door will open. The Lord's purpose will prevail!

Will you trust Him with your plans today?

Something to ponder:

1. Reflect on a time when a significant plan or goal you had didn't come to fruition. How did that experience shape your understanding of God's purpose in

your life, and what did you learn about trusting His plans over your own?

2. Consider your current plans and aspirations. How open are you to adjusting or surrendering these plans to align with what you perceive to be God's purpose for your life? What steps can you take to invite God's guidance and wisdom into your planning process?

CHAPTER EIGHT

DAY 8 - POWER SURGE FOR TODAY

PEACE IN SURRENDER!

"But whoever listens to me will live in safety and be at ease, without fear of harm."
Proverbs 1:33 NIV

Following advice and living at ease, without fear of harm - doesn't this make you really want to pay attention and listen to the advice from Solomon, the wisest man in the Bible?

It's hard for us to even imagine living in safety and being at ease, without fear, throughout our whole lives! That sounds so blissful. Solomon's words of wisdom throughout the book of Proverbs makes us realize that so often we bring on our own set of problems. If only we would listen and take his advice when making decisions, we would be far more at ease everyday.

Solomon tells us to watch our tongues and to keep our mouths shut so that we will stay out of trouble. Our tongues hold a lot of power, either to hurt and destroy or to do the opposite, to heal and restore. It's very easy then to see that our lives would be much more at ease if we were constantly following his advice to watch our tongue.

Solomon also tells us to trust God with our life and not to worry about the future. Trusting God with our life is probably what we struggle with the most. We seem to think we know better than God does.

Have you ever watched or been in a tug-of-war? It's fun to watch and to cheer for those tugging because it's human strength against human strength. But... we seem to be in a tug-of-war with God our whole life. We are not up against human strength in this tug-of-war, but against our omnipotent God and we are tugging for control. We are forever pulling and letting go, pulling hard and letting go again, until finally we surrender it all to God. Does this ring true in your life?

. . .

Our tug-of-war with God is not a game we are going to win. We may think we are for a time, but in the end, God wins and we will not be able to tug any longer. We will surrender to His will.

Let's give up our tug-of-war with God today and intentionally listen to the advice that Solomon is giving us today. Let's surrender our life to Him knowing that we can live at ease in the arms of Jesus, without fear of harm, as we totally depend on Him.

Something to ponder:

1. Reflect on a recent situation where failing to heed advice or being in a "tug-of-war" with God caused stress or complications in your life. What steps can you take to more willingly surrender and trust in God's guidance in similar circumstances moving forward?

2. Consider moments when you've experienced peace and safety by aligning your actions with wise counsel or God's guidance. How can you cultivate a habit of actively seeking and following advice, particularly when facing challenging decisions, to live more at ease and without fear of harm?

CHAPTER NINE

DAY 9 - POWER SURGE FOR TODAY

SHARED BURDENS!

"Carry each other's burdens, and in this way you will fulfill the law of Christ."
Galatians 6:2 NIV

We all have burdens that we carry around with us and they can weigh us down very quickly.

When was the last time you had a burden that weighed you down?

The meaning of the word burden means to carry a load, and usually it is a heavy load where help would certainly be appreciated. If you help to carry another person's load, you are fulfilling the law of Christ which is to love and serve one another. We are called to serve!

This reminds me of a camp mission in Northern Canada that requires a lot of manual labor to stack enough firewood each year. This mission relies on firewood for heat, both for cooking and for warmth, and they need about 12 to 16 cords of wood each winter to see them through to springtime. That's a lot of wood and it is a heavy burden for the leaders, as they do not have enough staff to fulfill this need.

A cord of wood, in case you don't know, is the amount of wood after being stacked and stowed, which measures approximately 4 feet high, by 8 feet long, by 4 feet deep. This is one cord of wood and the mission needs at least 12 cords of wood each winter! This burden feels overwhelming in itself, but when they don't have to carry the burden alone, the weight of the burden is suddenly lifted and the load is so much lighter.

Paul is instructing us to help carry each other's burdens. It is much easier when we don't have to go through difficult challenges and hardships alone. This may be carrying physical burdens, like helping with the firewood, or it may be helping to carry emotional burdens where we listen, share and pray together in times of grief or other emotional challenges. Being available to serve in these ways not only encourages us, but also helps others get through their difficult circumstances.

When we love in this way, we grow in empathy and in understanding of each other. This creates a closer bond with one another and can also create a special friendship through serving as Jesus calls us to do. It encourages us to keep going, to persevere and it fills our hearts with praise.

Carrying each other's burdens also serves as a reminder that we may be in need of help and support at some point in our lives. We would want others to come alongside us to help carry our burdens as well so that our load wouldn't weigh us down.

Do you have a burden that needs lifting today? Ask God to bring someone into your life to help carry your burden and lighten your load. If not, will you help to lift someone else's burden today?

Something to ponder:

1. Reflect on a time when someone helped you carry a burden, either physical or emotional. How did that act of support impact you, and how might you pay

that kindness forward by helping someone else with their burden?

2. Consider the burdens you currently carry, whether they're physical, emotional, or spiritual. How comfortable do you feel in asking for help or support from others? What steps could you take to both be willing to ask for assistance when needed and to be available to lend a helping hand to others in their time of need?

CHAPTER TEN

DAY 10 - POWER SURGE FOR TODAY

THE POWER OF WORDS!

"Let no corrupting talk come out of your mouths, but only such as is good for building up, as fits the occasion, that it may give grace to those who hear."

Ephesians 4:29 ESV

How often do we think about the words that are coming out of our mouths? Words can be very costly because once they are said, we cannot take them back. The damage is done!

This verse reminds us that our words have the power to build up or tear down. Words can tear down very quickly.

- Words can sting
- Words can hurt
- Words can cut
- Words can crush
- Words can stab
- Words can burn
- Words can harm
- Words can destroy

I'm sure you have been the recipient of some of these destructive words at some point in your life. Words can go deep and can bring us down quickly. Words can make us feel defeated and make us want to give up. Words hold a lot of power, so we need to be very careful with our words.

We also need to know how to counteract these destructive words when they are directed at us so that we do allow the enemy to defeat us. Speaking words of wisdom from God's truths and claiming His promises will help us fight the devil. Our identity comes from Jesus, not from words from the enemy trying to tear us down.

As believers in Jesus Christ, we are more than conquerors. We are called to use our words to build up and encourage others, which in turn will also build us up and fill us with truth and grace.

- Words can calm
- Words can heal
- Words can restore
- Words can free
- Words can rebuild
- Words can comfort
- Words can mend
- Words can bring rest

We can build others up by speaking words of love, truth and grace. The truth of God's word is very powerful, and when we speak words of truth and grace to others, we are sharing a piece of God's love with them. Words of truth can bring healing and freedom to those who hear it.

We should always be mindful of the people we are speaking to and choose our words accordingly. As we think about our words today, may we strive to have our words be seasoned with grace and filled with love and truth so that we build each other up and bring glory and honor to God.

How will you use your words today?

Something to ponder:

. . .

1. Reflect on a recent conversation where your words had a significant impact, positive or negative, on someone. How could you have adjusted your words to better align with the goal of building up and giving grace to the listener?

2. Consider a time when you were the recipient of uplifting or encouraging words. How did those words affect you, and how might you intentionally incorporate such positive language and encouragement into your own interactions with others today?

CHAPTER ELEVEN

DAY 11 - POWER SURGE FOR TODAY

CHOOSING YOUR ROAD!

"Enter through the narrow gate. For wide is the gate and broad is the road that leads to destruction, and many enter through it. But small is the gate and narrow the road that leads to life, and only a few find it."

Matthew 7:13-14 NIV

What a great analogy of our life. There are two roads and we get to choose which road we take. We can change lanes at any time too, if we so desire. If we are on the wide road, the narrow road is just an off-ramp away. If we are on the narrow road, the wide road is just an on-ramp away.

. . .

If we think about where both roads lead, either destruction or life, it's pretty clear which road we want to be on. Why would anyone even consider taking the road to destruction? And yet, this is the road that so many people are traveling on.

The wide road is easier and maybe even more comfortable. When the road is wide you have more space to veer to each side without fear of having an accident because it is broad. You can take more chances while driving on the broad road. For instance, you can take your eyes off the road for a few seconds longer and still stay on the road. You can turn around for a second or reach behind you to the back seat to grab something, or you can quickly text your friend. You can play with the radio, or you can daydream and let your mind wander a bit and still stay on the road. You can look out the window and enjoy the scenery more because you don't have to pay as much attention when you're on the wide road. But…it leads to destruction!

The narrow road is a more difficult highway to navigate. If you are driving on the narrow road you need to keep your eyes focused on the road ahead of you at all times. Taking your eyes off the road for just one second could mean you're on the shoulder taking the on-ramp to the wide road. The narrow road requires more intentional driving, but it leads to life!

. . .

It's so easy to get distracted and caught up with friends who are coaxing you to get into their vehicle heading down the wide road. Their weekend trip is so enticing and sounds so exciting. You could let your hair down and have some fun!

But...this kind of fun is only fun for a season and before you know it, the enticement is gone along with your integrity. Soon your values are not aligning with your heart and you are left feeling defeated. This is not the life you envisioned! The wide road leaves you feeling empty.

The narrow road may have some struggles and you may need to focus more, but it leads to life; a life of meaning, purpose and fulfillment. This is a road of ups and downs, of mountains and valleys, but Jesus rides the narrow road with us through every twist and turn, getting us through every weather pattern and every storm we encounter.

This verse says that only a few find the narrow road, even though it's the road that leads to life! This road will require us to be fully focused on Jesus because we can't drive the narrow road alone. When we are weak and tempted to take the on-ramp to the wide road, Jesus is our strength and He will take the wheel to keep us securely on the narrow road of life.

. . .

Let Jesus take the wheel today and He will keep you safe and secure.

Something to ponder:

1. Reflect on moments when you might have felt pulled towards the wider, more comfortable path in life. What were the circumstances, and how did you navigate your choices between the wider, easier route and the narrower, potentially more challenging path?

2. Consider a time when you actively chose the narrower, less traveled path in a decision or situation. How did that choice impact your life and your sense of purpose or fulfillment?

CHAPTER TWELVE

DAY 12 - POWER SURGE FOR TODAY

THE SOURCE ABOVE THE MOUNTAINS!

"I lift up my eyes to the mountains, where does my help come from? My help comes from the Lord, the Maker of heaven and earth."

Psalms 121:1-2 NIV

Sometimes we just don't recognize where our help comes from. We think we can do it alone, but we just can't!! We think we have enough will power, but we just don't. Our help comes from the Lord, so let's keep asking Him for help!

What are some things you need help with?

- Do you need help unpacking a trunk full of groceries?
- Do you need help changing the light bulbs in the ceiling?
- Do you need help painting the house?
- Do you need help taking out the garbage?
- Do you need help defrosting the deep-freeze?
- Do you need help getting the vehicle fixed?
- Do you need help getting your computer working?

You may have to do all those jobs by yourself because you have no one to help you with those tasks, but don't you think that when you ask God to help you even with these menial tasks, that he will give you the strength you need to actually accomplish getting them done? He helps your muscles work well for you. He gives you the strength to take one step at a time and get the job done, even if it takes longer than you wanted it to. He brings people into your path to help you if the job is too big for you. And...He gives you the ability to persevere and keep going until you accomplish the tasks on your to-do list.

But what about the impossible tasks that are not physical or manual labor jobs? We can't fix broken relationships alone. We can't take the grief of losing someone alone. We need to look up to the hills, which is where our help comes from. We can't take pain and sorrow away or speed up the time to mend our broken hearts. We need the strength from the Lord in order to get through these rough days.

Our help comes from looking up to the mountains. We need to look up above our eye level, above our glasses, above the tree line, because when we focus on the pain and hurt of what's directly in front of us, we will crumble. When our focus is on the struggle, it is too much for us to bear alone.

But...when we look up to the mountains, to the heavens, to the Lord...that is where our strength and help comes from. Will you look up today?

Here is a prayer for us today:

Oh God, we look up to the mountains right now. We know our help comes by looking up to you and we also know we can't do this journey alone. Today we ask that you give us the help we need to make it through another day and to be able to praise you through it! Give us the faith to trust you completely because we know that our help comes from you.

Help us to reclaim our health in our mind, our body, and our soul so that we can live out the purpose you have set out for us to do. Help us to see the opportunities that you put in front of us and give us the confidence to step out to use the gifts you have given us. Help us live our life solely focused on you today, and we trust that you will use us even when we are weak, because when we are weak, you are strong.

God, we know you are the maker of heaven and earth and You are all-powerful, so we ask that you would empower us right now to fight the enemy. Give us a strong mind to fight the lies from the devil. We pray that you would fill us with your power so that our doubt evaporates, and give us the joy of the Lord as we claim your promises. We trust that you will help us persevere to run our race well. In Jesus' name, Amen.

My Help Comes From The Lord!!

Something to ponder:

1. Reflect on a moment when you felt overwhelmed by a task or situation that seemed insurmountable. Did you seek help from external sources or rely solely on your own abilities? How might turning to God for help have changed the outcome or your perspective?

. . .

2. Think about instances when you felt strengthened or empowered during difficult times by seeking guidance or support from a higher power. How did this experience shape your understanding of seeking help from God in challenging situations?

CHAPTER THIRTEEN

DAY 13 - POWER SURGE FOR TODAY

OVERCOMING FEELINGS!

"I will give thanks to you, Lord, with all my heart; I will tell of all your wonderful deeds. I will be glad and rejoice in you; I will sing the praises of your name, O Most High."

Psalm 9:1-2 NIV

We don't always "feel" like praising the Lord and giving thanks, but we are supposed to do it anyway. Our feelings get in the way so often and really hold us back from doing what we know we should.

- We feel like eating our emotions rather than dealing with the root cause of our emotions

- We feel like being grumpy when things don't go our way rather than being flexible
- We feel like being angry at someone rather than forgiving them
- We feel like lying on the couch to watch a show rather than exercising
- We feel like buying junk food rather than making healthy food
- We feel like ignoring what God is asking us to do rather than stepping out and doing it
- We feel like giving up because it's hard rather than seeking God's strength to see us through

Feelings get in the way of being thankful or joyful so often. When we think about it logically, we know that we should not always rely on our feelings because often they are just not true. We know in our minds that feelings are not facts, but feelings are powerful.

Here's an example you will probably relate to. I've had a very bad cough recently and I know that Buckley's cough syrup tastes horrible, but it works! I don't feel like taking it, but the fact is that I know it will help me stop coughing. So what do I do? I rely on the facts over my feelings and just take the dreaded spoonful of medicine.

. . .

No matter if your road is hard or easy, long or short, challenging or smooth-sailing, God always calls us to rejoice in Him. The fact is that we have a lot to be thankful for and we can rejoice even when our feelings tell us the opposite.

If you are struggling to rejoice today, think about some of these wonderful facts:

- Jesus died for me to give me life everlasting
- Jesus understands all my feelings
- Jesus knows my heart
- Jesus gets my pain
- Jesus is my comfort
- Jesus gives me strength
- Jesus accepts me as I am
- Jesus loves me unconditionally

Let's keep fighting to rejoice in the Lord and not let our feelings take us down. Today let's tell of His wonderful deeds; Jesus is our rock and our fortress and He will deliver us from the enemy.

Something to ponder:

1. Reflect on a time when your feelings conflicted with your understanding of what you knew was right

or beneficial. How did you navigate this conflict between emotions and logic? What did you learn from that experience?

2. Think about a recent situation where you chose to act based on facts or convictions rather than succumbing to your immediate feelings. How did this decision impact the outcome or your perspective on the situation?

CHAPTER FOURTEEN

DAY 14 - POWER SURGE FOR TODAY

FINDING FREEDOM

"Submit yourselves, then, to God. Resist the devil, and he will flee from you."

James 4:7 NIV

There are two action words in this verse and James is giving us a huge life lesson here. He first tells us that we need to submit ourselves. In the dictionary the word submit means "to accept or yield to a superior force or to the authority or will of another person." James specifically says we are to yield to God. God is our supreme authority and James is commanding us to accept this.

. . .

Why do we find it so difficult to submit to God? We know He loves us and wants the best for us, so why do we want to rebel against Him? If we think of our own children, we love them and want the very best for them. God loves us even more than we love our own children; in fact, we can't even imagine how much He truly loves us. He wants the best for us too, so why do we think we can do it our own way?

If we think about a trial going on in a courthouse, we know that the defendant must submit to the ruling of the judge. The defendant must yield or pay the consequences of not submitting to authority. In essence, this is what James is telling us. We need to submit to God, because He is our ultimate authority.

There is, however, one major difference between a judge in a courtroom and God. The judge did not lay down his life and die for the defendant; God's unconditional love for the defendant can never be matched.

James goes on to tell us that we must also resist the devil! To resist means to "withstand the action or effect of" or to "refrain from doing or having." Even though the devil prowls around like a roaring lion, we must not let Him have authority over us; we must refrain from doing what he is tempting us to do.

. . .

What aspect of your life has the enemy been tempting you with? If you were in God's courtroom today, what is He asking you to submit to Him? Is it your hobby, your family, your weight-loss journey, your financial situation?

It's time we submit and surrender our "All" to God, not just one or two aspects of our life, but every aspect of our journey. Let's yield to the one who wants the very best for us and who gave His life for us so that we could live.

God is patient and loving and gives us the freedom to choose. God is not going to bang the gavel on the desk like the judge in a courthouse, but He lovingly calls us to submit and obey. We know that God's way is the best way, so let's resist the devil and choose to submit to God. This is true freedom in Christ.

Something to ponder:

1. Reflect on a time when you resisted a temptation or an influence that was not aligned with your values or beliefs. How did this experience affect your relationship with God or your sense of spiritual strength?

2. Are there areas in your life where you struggle to yield to God's guidance or authority? What might be

holding you back from submitting those aspects of your life to God's will?

CHAPTER FIFTEEN

DAY 15 - POWER SURGE FOR TODAY

Embracing Faith Over Doubt

"But when you ask, you must believe and not doubt, because the one who doubts is like a wave of the sea, blown and tossed by the wind."

James 1:6 NIV

Believing without doubt is like planting a seed in good, nutrient-dense soil and waiting for it to grow. You have no doubt that it will grow strong and flourish because the seed has everything it needs to grow. Doubting is like planting a seed in hard, rocky soil and waiting for it to do nothing. You doubt it will grow strong because it has no nourishment to sustain it so it will struggle to take root.

. . .

I remember a time when I set out on a vacation to do some hiking with my friends. I was nervous and doubted my ability to climb this great mountain. My friends were long-time hikers, and I was not used to climbing mountains. I had heard about their wonderful stories of the breathtaking views from the summits and the sense of accomplishment that came with reaching the top, but I doubted my ability to climb this 9000 foot mountain with them. My doubts prevailed.

The day came when my friends and I set out on our journey for this climb. It was a beautiful, bluebird day and I decided not to let the doubts and fear hold me back from enjoying the beauty of God's creation. I could let my mind wander to the fear I have of bears, both black bears and grizzly bears in this habitat, or I could rest in knowing that I was hiking with experienced hikers who knew how to avoid going near the bears.

As we neared the summit and were tired from the climb, we also felt exhilarated with being on top of the world, experiencing God's exquisite creation. At the top of the mountain we could look down and see the valleys below. We could see things we had never seen before and look down on all the obstacles we had overcome to get to where we were standing now.

· · ·

I could have let doubt and fear hold me back, but I would have missed out on experiencing the joy that comes from being on God's mountaintop, which was an experience of a lifetime!

Our doubts often hold us back in our journey of life. Our fears often prevent us from living a life of meaning and fulfillment and from experiencing God's mountaintop. Our doubts can make us feel like a wave of the sea, being tossed about by the winds of life.

Pushing through our doubts and fears can give us a newfound confidence to keep pressing forward to meet our goals. When we put one foot in front of the other, with each step forward we can reach the summit. Pressing on with determination causes our doubt to dissipate as we lean into the strength from the Lord, knowing that with Him we can tackle any challenge that comes our way.

Let's thank God for His faithfulness and give all our doubts and fears to Him right now. Today we will not be like a wave, tossed and jostled around by the wind because when we walk with God, we don't have to doubt. We just Believe!

Something to ponder:

. . .

1. Reflect on a time when doubt hindered you from taking a significant step forward. How did you overcome that doubt or what steps could you take to navigate doubt differently in the future?

2. Are there specific areas in your life where doubt tends to dominate your decision-making or actions? How might leaning on faith instead of doubt impact those areas positively?

CHAPTER SIXTEEN

DAY 16 - POWER SURGE FOR TODAY

UNFATHOMABLE PEACE!

"Peace I leave with you; my peace I give you. I do not give to you as the world gives. Do not let your hearts be troubled and do not be afraid."

John 14:27 NIV

Peace - what words or thoughts come to your mind when you think of peace? Do you think about resting and listening to a meditation, or do you think of lying on a sandy beach in the tropical sun, or are you listening to soothing spa music as you relax through a massage? What words describe peace to you?

In the dictionary, peace is described as "freedom from disturbance, tranquility, or a period of no war."

But...Jesus says He gives us a different kind of peace; not like the world gives! So what kind of peace is this?

I was recently in a situation where I felt there was some conflict between myself and another person. Words were taken out of context and feelings soared high. I'm sure you can relate to a scenario like this in your life at some point, and when this happens there seems to be no peace!

We can apologize for our part in the conflict, for harsh words that may have transpired or for actions that were misunderstood, but there is not always reconciliation in these situations. So then how do we experience peace?

As I got in the shower that morning, I felt God's blessing of peace wash over my heart just like the hot water washed over my body. I was reminded to pray for this person, and to just allow the Holy Spirit to perform His work in both of us and His peace washed over me like the rain from the shower. As we commune with God, a peace is given to us that is not like the world gives, but an inner peace that floods our hearts.

Have you experienced His peace or do you long for it?

. . .

Not every scenario works out the way we expect it to. We don't always experience reconciliation because this takes both parties desiring to reconcile. But we can always experience the peace that God gives us, even in these troubling times. His peace can permeate our soul and we do not have to be troubled because we know that God will work all things out for good in due time.

Jesus tells us in this verse that we should not be troubled or afraid. Even through conflict or disturbances or trouble, we do not have to be afraid because God is faithful and He will be our strength in times of trouble.

We are not promised a garden of roses and sunshine throughout our life, but we are promised peace even among the storms and rains that come.

Whatever you are troubled with today, allow God to bless you with His peace which is so different from that of the world. The old hymn, *Great Is Thy Faithfulness*, says it perfectly.

Pardon for sin and a peace that endureth
Thine own dear presence to cheer and to guide
Strength for today and bright hope for tomorrow

Blessings all mine with 10,000 beside

Great is Thy faithfulness
Great is Thy faithfulness
Morning by morning new mercies I see
All I have needed Thy hand hath provided
Great is Thy faithfulness
Great is Thy faithfulness
Great is Thy faithfulness, Lord, unto me

Prayer for Today:

God, today we ask for your Peace that is beyond comprehension! We know that it's possible to have peace in our rocky situations, but our minds take us to the doubts and fears. Lord, we lift up our thoughts to You and ask for help in keeping our thoughts on things that are pure and good and patient and kind. We give you our troubles right now and ask that you give us wisdom to know what to do so that we will experience your peace through the storms of life. Thank you for your great faithfulness and for the new mercies that you give us each morning.

In Jesus name, AMEN.

Something to ponder:

. . .

1. Can you recall a moment when you experienced a profound sense of peace in a troubling situation? What factors or actions contributed to that peace during that time?

2. When facing conflicts or disturbances, how do you typically seek peace? Are there new approaches or perspectives you might consider to access the peace that God offers, even in challenging circumstances?

CHAPTER SEVENTEEN

DAY 17 - POWER SURGE FOR TODAY

EMPOWERED OVERCOMERS!

"You, dear children are from God and have overcome them, because the one who is in you is greater than the one who is in the world."

1 John 4:4 NIV

This verse is Powerful!! If we believe the Bible to be true, which as believers we claim to believe, then we must also believe that the power in us is greater than the power that is in the world. Do you truly believe this?

You have probably heard before that there are only really these three options: Jesus was either deluded, so a lunatic, or He was a fraud, so a con-man, or He is the Truth - The Messiah!

As believers, we do believe He is the Way, The Truth and The Life! He really is who He says He is - WOW! This also means that because we have the power living within us, the devil has to flee! The enemy holds no power over us because greater is He who is in us than he who is in the world. We claim victory in Jesus!

This victory sounds so empowering, yet so often we don't even think about using this amazing power within us. This power is ours to use and ours to go into battle with, whether it's a battle in our minds, thoughts, doubts and fears, or whether it's a battle with our actions and reactions, or whether it's a battle with an addiction or an obsession, or a battle with food or alcohol temptation, or a battle in a relationship... and the list goes on.

Which giant battle do you need to overcome today? Are you facing the giant of Fear, Failure, Self-Sabotage, Discouragement, Insecurity, Procrastination, Distraction, Rejection, or Time? These are real giants in our world today, but only because we allow them to overtake us. Jesus promises that we have the power to overcome.

. . .

We are Children of God, made in the Image of God, equipped with the Power of God. Let's go out and slay our giants today and be overcomers with God!

Something to ponder:

1. What aspects of your life or situations challenge your belief of the power within you? How can you actively tap into this power during those challenging times?

2. Are there areas in your life where you've underestimated the strength and authority you have as a child of God? How might acknowledging this power within influence your approach to overcoming difficulties?

CHAPTER EIGHTEEN

DAY 18 - POWER SURGE FOR TODAY

FRUITFUL LIVING!

"By their fruit you will recognize them. Do people pick grapes from thornbushes, or figs from thistles?"

Matthew 7:16 NIV

When you think of fruit, do you think of people's characteristics or their personalities? How do you recognize people by their fruit?

Quite literally, we do not look at a person eating an apple and judge them by what fruit they are eating! For instance, this person is eating a green apple so they must be very smart. That person is eating a red apple so they must be really wealthy, and another person is eating a yellow apple so they must be very spiritual! This sounds absurd, right?

So what does this verse mean? We hear a lot about the fruits of the spirit and about producing good fruit or bad fruit, and recognizing people by their fruit.

Jesus has great stories and great analogies that we can learn from and the fruit of the spirit are all characteristics that we strive to produce in our lives. Just like fruit takes time to grow on trees, so do these characteristics take time to grow in our lives.

When we see a person who is prickly, rude and harsh, we truly don't expect to be shown kindness from them. We don't pick grapes from a thornbush because the law of reaping and sowing doesn't allow for that, and this law comes from the Lord.

When we think of reaping what we sow, we do not harvest corn when we plant peas. It's the same in our own lives. If we choose to sow a life of misery, conflict, bitterness, corruption and rebellion, we will definitely not produce a life of love, joy, kindness, patience and self-control. We do not reap peace when we plant hatred.

. . .

Jesus tells us that we will be able to recognize or identify His followers by their fruits. Fruits are a common metaphor that we can relate to; they are spoken about in both the Old and New Testaments. They represent the outward expression of our behavior and our actions to the world, representing that we are followers of Jesus.

By living our everyday normal life, we are called to be a representation of Jesus, producing the characteristics or fruit of the spirit, so that those around us would see Jesus in us. The question to ask ourselves is this: Do people see us as a thornbush with thistles or as a fig tree with delicious fruit?

In this journey of life, we are continually developing the fruits of the spirit so that others may recognize us. Somedays our fruit is not recognizable or it has become rotten fruit. But God, with His loving patience and grace, shows us new mercies every morning. He continues to fertilize and water us so that little by little our fruit becomes evident.

Let's not give up, but rather let's thank the Lord for not giving up on us. What fruit will we produce today?

Something to ponder:

. . .

1. Reflecting on your recent interactions or behaviors, what "fruit" have you been displaying in your life? How might these traits align with the values you strive to uphold?

2. Are there specific areas in your life where you feel your "fruit" needs improvement or refinement? What steps can you take to nurture these characteristics to better reflect your beliefs and values?

CHAPTER NINETEEN

DAY 19 - POWER SURGE FOR TODAY

A Profound Gift!

"But to each one of us grace has been given as Christ apportioned it."

Ephesians 4:7 NIV

What is grace and why do we need it?

An easy definition that I found for the meaning of biblical grace was "approval or kindness, that is freely given by God to all humans." Grace is given to us without merit; we did nothing to receive God's goodness or kindness.

. . .

One winter night around New Years, my hubby and I decided we would like to take our whole family out for dinner. This is quite an ordeal, as there are five grandchildren ranging from one year of age all the way up to 12 years of age, and we are 13 people in total. Trying to organize a time where we can all get together at the same time, in the same place, definitely takes some organizing.

We made a reservation and we all arrived at the restaurant eager to spend a wonderful time eating together, visiting, and just enjoying each other's company. After a great evening with family, as we were getting ready to leave and pay the bill, we had the biggest surprise of our life. The server came over and explained to us that someone had just paid for our whole entire family dinner! This seemed too good to be true - this was a big deal!

This was not someone "paying it forward" with a coffee, but paying it forward with a dinner that cost hundreds of dollars. I want to say that this was an act of kindness shown to our family that was totally unmerited and very unexpected.

This is what I would call unmerited grace, something we did not deserve. We hadn't done anything honorable, we hadn't done anything especially nice for anyone that day, we didn't even know the people who paid for our bill; this was purely an act of kindness!

The beautiful gesture shown to us that night was such a wonderful reminder of God's unmerited love and grace for us. God's grace is given to us freely; He aportions it to us. We don't deserve God's grace and there is nothing we can do to deserve it.

AND...God's grace far surpasses this beautiful act of kindness shown to us that night. This is a beautiful reminder for us that we need to be showing grace to others. There is nothing that comes even close to God's divine, appointed grace.

God's grace is sufficient for us at all times and He knows how many times we will need an extra dose of grace. His unmerited favor on us is something supernatural. He knows our journey and He has apportioned out the grace we need, and it is sufficient!

As you ponder on the grace you have been shown, without merit, allow yourself to bask in the goodness of God and all the blessings He bestows upon you. Let's receive His love gracefully and remember to show grace to others in return.

Something to ponder:

. . .

1. Reflecting on moments where unexpected kindness or grace was extended to you, how did that impact your perception of grace and its significance in your life?

2. In what ways can you intentionally extend grace or kindness to others, even in situations where it might not be expected or earned?

CHAPTER TWENTY

DAY 20 - POWER SURGE FOR TODAY

LIVING BY DESIGN!

"But whoever looks intently into the perfect law that gives freedom, and continues in it - not forgetting what they have heard, but doing it they will be blessed in what they do."

James 1:25 NIV

This verse reminds us of the importance of truly understanding and living out the word of God. It is not enough to simply hear or read the Bible, but we must take the time to study it and apply it to our lives. When we do this, we will find true freedom in living according to God's perfect blueprint for our lives.

. . .

Looking intently means to look with great effort, in a concentrated manner or with laser focus. This makes me think of times when we look intently in a magnified mirror and we are laser focused on our face, concentrating so intensely to find the one particular hair that needs to be removed. I know this seems rather comical, but it certainly shows how intently we can focus on something so small and insignificant, yet how so often we neglect to focus that intently on the word of God!

When we think of a blueprint for best living, we think of a guide for our life with a specific design or pattern of living that can be followed with intention. The best example I can think of is a blueprint for a custom house. This is a set of papers which holds a blue set of carefully drawn out designs or construction plans that will help a contractor build that specific house. When the plans are followed closely, carefully and intentionally, that specific house will be the blessing or the result.

The word of God is also a specific set of guidelines for us to live intentionally so that we live our best life. Our body is a temple, so following God's blueprint to build our temple to be the best it can be makes a lot of sense. God's blueprint for living is designed for us individually just like a blueprint for a custom designed house.

. . .

Additionally, this verse also highlights the importance of consistency in living out our faith. We are told to continue in the word, not forgetting what we have learned, but instead to put it into practice in our daily lives. When we do this, we will be blessed in all that we do.

Let's take time to study the word of God intently and then learn to apply it to our own life each day. As we learn to practice this daily habit, we will find true freedom and experience the blessings that come from living intentionally by the word of God, our blueprint for best living.

Something to ponder:

1. How can you improve your focus and intentionality in studying and applying the teachings from the Bible in your daily life?

2. Reflecting on moments when you've applied biblical principles to your life, what blessings or positive changes have you experienced as a result?

CHAPTER TWENTY-ONE

DAY 21 - POWER SURGE FOR TODAY

UNWAVERING ETERNAL LOVE!

"For God so loved the world that he gave his one and only Son, that whoever believes in him shall not perish but have eternal life."

John 3:16 NIV

Because this verse is so well-known and we have heard it so many times, we often seem to dismiss it quickly. Quite frankly, it rolls off our tongue too easily and sometimes feels like just another slogan like Nike's slogan - Just Do It!

This verse really summarizes the message of love and salvation that is at the core of our faith. It tells us that God loves the world so much that He was willing to give His only son, Jesus, to save us from our sins and offer us eternal life.

It seems that people today do not feel like they need saving from anything. Many people feel they are invincible, they can do it on their own strength, they don't need help from their neighbors, and they certainly don't need saving from something they don't believe in - eternal life!

Despite all our flaws and imperfections, God's incredible love is still given to us freely; in fact, it is so deep and so powerful that God is willing to make the ultimate sacrifice so that we can live forever with Him. The word says we will not perish, meaning that we really never die even after our physical bodies have passed away. We go from life on earth to everlasting life with Jesus. It's almost surreal; we can't really fathom this amazing supernatural departure from this earth.

It was Billy Graham, the biggest evangelist of the 20th century who said, "Someday you will read or hear that Billy Graham is dead. Don't you believe a word of it. I shall be more alive than I am now. I will just have changed my address. I will have gone into the presence of God."

. . .

It is important to remember that, although this is one of the most well-known verses in the Bible, it is not one that we want to quickly pass over without pondering. God tells us of His great love for us, but then He also gives us a call to action that we cannot take lightly. This is not just a nice sentiment, but it is an invitation to believe in Jesus and to follow Him, so that we may have eternal life.

It is also a reminder that we are not alone in this world, no matter what situation we find ourselves in. We may be struggling with loneliness, depression, anxiety, not knowing what our future holds, but we do know that we have a loving God who is always with us, guiding and protecting us and if we believe, this is a great reminder that through Jesus, we can have hope and peace, even in the midst of difficult times.

Let us never forget the amazing love of God and the sacrifice of Jesus poured out for you and I. Every single human on this earth craves love and hope, and we know that in Him, we have the deepest love that anyone could give which gives us the greatest hope that anyone could have.

Let's thank God today for His unwavering love that allows us to go from this life on earth to life everlasting with Him and never die.

. . .

Remember, God LOVES You!

Something to ponder:

1. How does the depth of God's love, as described in this verse, impact your perspective on life and your relationships with others?

2. Reflecting on your beliefs and faith journey, how has the promise of eternal life through Jesus influenced the way you approach challenges and uncertainties in your life?

CHAPTER TWENTY-TWO

DAY 22 - POWER SURGE FOR TODAY

GOD'S CONSTANT PRESENCE!

"God is our refuge and strength, an ever-present help in trouble."

Psalms 46:1 NIV

Simple Truth! Clear Truth!

Simple Message! Clear Message!

Simple Promise! Clear Promise!

God's words are powerful, yet simple and clear so that anyone who reads the Word of God can understand His message. We may not be scholars or theologians and understand how all the pieces of history align with prophecy, but God does speak clearly to each individual through His word as it is living and active to everyone who receives it.

This verse reminds us of the strength and protection that God provides for us in times of trouble and gives us great hope during times of distress. No matter what we may be facing, we know that God is always there to provide us with the protection and guidance that we need.

God says He is our ever-present help. This is one of the most comforting aspects of knowing God, just to know that He is always with us, ever-present. We can't really fathom what this truly means because when we think of our closest friend or spouse, they cannot always be with us. They cannot always help us in our times of difficulty. And very often, they don't really know how to comfort us when we need them the most!

But God, our strength and our protection, is ever-present. Always with us. Always there. Always understanding. Always present. Nothing could be more reassuring or comforting than this!

So what trouble are you facing? Trouble looks different for each person.

. . .

It could look like this:

- Financial trouble
- Car trouble
- Family relationship trouble
- Time management trouble
- Disorganization or mess trouble
- Busyness of life trouble
- Loneliness trouble
- Children trouble
- Anxiety trouble
- Pain trouble
- Emotional trouble

It is very easy, when we are in trouble, to lose sight of God's presence and we feel so alone. There are so many kinds of trouble, but God tells us that He is our strength and our ever-present help for all our troubles, not just occasionally. We are never alone and He is always waiting to guide us and to help us navigate through difficult times.

And...let's not forget that even when we are not in trouble, God is still ever-present! He is always working in our lives, regardless of the situation, waiting to be our guide and to help us in the way we need Him most.

. . .

This is a powerful reminder to turn to Him at all times, and to trust in His protection and His guidance in our lives. He wants the best for us, so let's give Him our best and trust His presence with us.

Something to ponder:

1. Reflecting on past challenges, how has the awareness of God's ever-present help influenced your approach to overcoming difficulties?

2. In which areas of your life do you find it most challenging to trust that God is an ever-present help? How might acknowledging His presence in those specific areas bring comfort or change your perspective?

CHAPTER TWENTY-THREE

DAY 23 - POWER SURGE FOR TODAY

THE TRANSFORMATIVE MELODY!

"He put a new song in my mouth, a hymn of praise to our God. Many will see and fear the Lord and put their trust in him."

Psalms 40:3 NIV

When we put our trust in God, there is a transforming power within us that gives us a new song. This is a new song of joy, peace and such great hope for the future. This new song is a reflection of the change that Jesus brings about in our hearts as we trust in Him.

When I think of a reflection, I think of standing beside a shimmering lake, with the sun rays reflecting the beauty of the mountain side along with all the glorious colors of the fall trees, and I cannot decipher what is real and what is not. The reflection is so bright and vivid, there is no way to know which one is real.

Our lives should be this kind of a vivid reflection of Jesus so that others are drawn to the Lord because they see Jesus working through us. This is the kind of new song we want to share with others, not by our own power, but by the power of God at work in us.

Imagine a world-renowned musician who is known for his beautiful melodies. Yet one day he wakes up with a new song in his heart, one that is vastly different from anything he's ever written before. This new song is filled with joy, hope and love, and he cannot help but share it with the world.

As he performs this new song, people are drawn to it. They can feel the love. They can feel the joy in their heart. They can feel the hope in their spirit. They are moved by the message it conveys. Before long this new song becomes a hit, and people all over the world are singing it.

Just like this musician, when God puts a new song in our hearts, it has the power to change those we come in contact with. Our new song will be contagious and others will be drawn to the love, joy and peace that is reflected through our song.

Let us embrace this new song that God has put in our mouths and let it be a testimony to His transformative power in our lives. Let us sing and shout this new song with joy and gratitude, and let it be a light that shines in the darkness and brings hope to those around us.

Something to ponder:

1. Reflecting on your own journey, what moments or changes have occurred that brought about a "new song" in your life, spiritually or emotionally? How did this impact your interactions with others?

2. Are there areas in your life where you feel the need for a "new song," a sense of renewal or a fresh perspective? How might embracing God's transformative power in those areas impact your relationships and interactions?

CHAPTER TWENTY-FOUR

DAY 24 - POWER SURGE FOR TODAY

SEEKING GOD'S KINGDOM!

"But seek first his kingdom and his righteousness, and all these things will be given to you as well."
Matthew 6:33 NIV

What does it mean to seek? When I think of seeking, I think of researching on the internet. I love looking at vacation spots and seeking out the best place for my husband and I to go, someplace warm with a nice beach, good food, and just a great place to relax. I usually keep searching and seeking until I find the perfect place for our holiday and then show my hubby what I found.

. . .

I also remember when my children were little, if they lost a special toy or something that was part of a toy set, I would seek for that item until it was found. Sometimes I found it quickly, and other times it took me days, but I kept seeking!

But seeking God's kingdom and His righteousness does not have an end time. You don't find it and then stop seeking. Each day we are to seek and we should never stop seeking! This takes on a whole new meaning!

So what does this mean? I started seeking (on Google) what it means to seek God's kingdom and the best definition I could find was that God's kingdom is the realm where Jesus' authority is acknowledged and obeyed. To seek God's kingdom and His righteousness is to obey Him in three realms; 1) to obey Him within our own life, 2) to obey Him in our circle of immediate influence, and 3) to obey Him as far around the world as we can reach.

When we seek to obey God in all three realms, this really encompasses our whole life and the great commission of spreading the gospel. When we are seeking to be under the authority of God and when we allow Him to be in control of our life, then we are living under the kingdom of God. It is not a bunch of rules and regulations, but rather the freedom of seeking to live with the peace and joy that comes from trusting Him.

When we do seek His kingdom and His righteousness first, Jesus promises that all the things we need will be given to us so we will not have to worry about how our next need is met. When we seek God, we will find the answers and He will provide for our needs, but we do need to keep seeking Him!

Just as a host provides for their guests, so God always provides for those who seek Him. So let's remember to seek God first in our lives today, above all else, and trust that He will provide for all our needs and bless us in ways we can't even imagine.

Something to ponder:

1. Reflecting on your daily life, how often do you consciously seek to align your actions and decisions with God's authority and teachings in the three realms mentioned—personal life, immediate circle of influence, and broader impact? What adjustments could you make to seek His kingdom more intentionally in each of these areas?

. . .

2. When faced with a situation or decision, what practices or habits do you employ to seek God's guidance and prioritize His kingdom and righteousness? Are there moments when seeking God first has resulted in unexpected outcomes or blessings?

CHAPTER TWENTY-FIVE

DAY 25 - POWER SURGE FOR TODAY

EMBRACING DIVINE POWER!

"His divine power has given us everything we need for a godly life through our knowledge of him who called us by his own glory and goodness."

2 Peter 1:3 NIV

So often I wish I had everything I needed to do a certain task or to start a new thing. I get ready to make a new recipe and I realize I am missing one ingredient and have to rush to the store before I can begin. Or maybe I want to create a new project and I don't have the right color of paper or paint to complete it. I feel like I need something different or I'm lacking some supplies.

. . .

We may not always have everything we need to complete certain projects, but we know where we can go to get them. However, we do always have everything we need to live for Jesus, to live a godly life, and to live out the purpose He has designed for us daily. His divine power has given us exactly what we need.

Sometimes though, we still feel like we are lacking things; we feel like we lack wisdom to make the right decision or we feel like we lack strength to persevere. Maybe we feel like we lack joy or peace in a stressful situation. It's so easy to feel like we don't have everything we need and that we can't make it through life's challenges, but those feelings are lies and doubts coming from the enemy. This verse says we do have everything we need. We have His divine power!

This makes me think of my husband's toolbox. His garage is filled with a whole bunch of tools in his toolbox because he needs a lot of different tools to fix different vehicles. Just like his toolbox contains all the power tools he needs to complete his mechanical jobs, God's divine power source provides us with everything we need in our spiritual toolbox.

Our knowledge of God (the Word) is the key to our toolbox and it unlocks all the resources He has given us to live a life that pleases Him. Just as my husband selects the right tool out of his toolbox in the garage, we also must choose the right tool out of our spiritual toolbox for the task we are working on. We must continually choose the right tools to make it through the struggles and temptations that come our way.

It's not enough to just own the toolbox; the tools actually have to be taken out and used! Are you using the tools in your spiritual toolbox or are you keeping them hidden beneath the lid? To have the knowledge and to keep it locked up in a toolbox is such a waste of a resource. Let's stop wasting the spiritual resources we have been given and start using the tools to help us move forward in our daily walk with God.

When we truly know God and understand His nature, we are given a sense of peace, joy and strength that surpasses all understanding. This knowledge also gives us wisdom and understanding, helping us to navigate our own life's challenges with God's grace and confidence.

The more we use the tools we have been given, the more comfortable we will get using them. It may feel somewhat scary or uncomfortable to use a new power tool at first, but with practice and daily consistency they will soon feel natural in your hands. In the same way, using the spiritual tools will also become easier and more comfortable with practice and consistency and soon you will realize that His divine power is everything you need.

Praying you have the Divine Power You Need Today.

Something to ponder:

1. Reflect on the spiritual tools or resources you possess. Which ones do you find yourself frequently using in navigating life's challenges? Are there tools or aspects of your spiritual knowledge you haven't utilized yet that could be helpful in your daily walk?

2. When facing difficulties or feeling inadequate, how often do you consciously turn to the spiritual tools at your disposal, such as prayer, Scripture, or spiritual practices, to access God's divine power? How might incorporating these tools more consistently impact your sense of peace, strength, and wisdom in challenging situations?

CHAPTER TWENTY-SIX

DAY 26 - POWER SURGE FOR TODAY

CULTIVATING JOY!

"Rejoice in the Lord always. I will say it again: Rejoice!"

Philippians 4:4 NIV

If you're like me, you probably find that it's easy to read this verse and rejoice when things are going well, but when the tough times come it's not that easy to rejoice in our circumstances. It's a whole lot easier to become negative and to grumble and complain.

As we begin our day, let's consider what it means to rejoice in the Lord always! It's easy to get caught up in the busyness of life and to forget the importance of cultivating joy in our hearts, but this is what we are told to do. This doesn't mean we have to do the happy dance every morning, but what it does mean is that we need to start our day with a joyful heart. It means we need to get into a mindset of thanksgiving so that we have something to be joyful about.

If we think about a fruit tree planted near a river, the roots of the tree have grown deep and wide, continually drawing from the constant supply of refreshing water provided by the river. The leaves of the tree are always green and full, and the fruit is abundant and pleasing to the eye. The tree exudes life, joy and contentment because of its nourishment.

We can imagine ourselves like this tree, planted by the river. We draw from the constant supply of joy that comes from being connected to the Lord, and as a result, our lives are marked by fruitfulness and the joy of the Lord. When we have this constant supply of refreshing living water, then we always have something to rejoice in, even when things are not going as planned.

But just like a tree needs to be planted in the right soil, we too need to be planted in the right soil. We need to cultivate our relationship with the Lord in order to experience the fullness of joy that comes from being in his presence. This means taking the time to pray, to be thankful, taking time to read the Bible and to meditate on God's goodness.

So today let's remember the importance of rejoicing in the Lord always. Let's take a few moments to pause, reflect, and to give thanks for all that the Lord has done for us. Rather than having a grumbling spirit or being like a wilting tree with dull fruit, let's allow our hearts to be filled with joy so that our fruit will be vibrant, just like the tree planted by the river.

May you find joy today in serving Jesus.

Something to ponder:

1. Reflect on a recent challenging situation. How did your initial response align with rejoicing in the Lord always? Did you find it challenging to maintain a joyful perspective during difficulties, or did you manage to find elements of gratitude or trust in God's provision within the situation?

2. Consider your daily spiritual routine. How consistently do you engage in practices that cultivate joy and gratitude in your life, such as prayer, thanksgiving, or meditation on God's goodness? Are there

adjustments you could make to nourish your spiritual life more intentionally, leading to a more consistent state of rejoicing in the Lord?

CHAPTER TWENTY-SEVEN

DAY 27 - POWER SURGE FOR TODAY

TRUSTING GOD'S GPS!

"Do not be anxious about anything, but in every situation, by prayer and petition, with thanksgiving, present your requests to God."

Philippians 4:6 NIV

It's so very easy to become anxious about decisions we need to make or about circumstances we are going through, and yet anxiety is something we don't want to suffer with because it can be so debilitating. Anxiety is very bad for our health so it's no wonder that God's word tells us not to be anxious about anything, but to petition God on our behalf.

. . .

To petition God means to formally ask God for a request, and oftentimes, formal requests are presented in writing. Giving our requests to Him is not something to be taken lightly; this verse tells us to give God our requests (in writing or in prayer) and when we obey this simple command, it will help us not to become anxious.

Trusting God with my requests makes me think about a GPS device. If I don't know how to get somewhere, it's so easy to enter the destination into a GPS to help guide me to the right place. I put my complete trust in the GPS device to get me where I want to go. Why is it that I can trust my man-made device, yet I so often doubt God's guidance in my own life?

God is so much more trustworthy than a GPS! God loves us and wants to have fellowship with us. He really cares about our journey and wants us to bring our requests, with thanksgiving, to Him. We can trust Him to guide us on the right path completely, not only with big life decisions, but also with our thoughts and worries so that anxiety doesn't overtake us. We can bring all our fears and anxious thoughts to Him and petition God on our behalf. His GPS will guide us and provide us with the peace that we so desperately need.

. . .

Next time you feel overwhelmed with worries, take a moment to pause and present your requests to God in prayer. Trust that He hears you and will guide you on the right path, and remember to give thanks in every situation, knowing that God is working in your life for your good and for His glory.

Something to ponder:

1. Reflect on a recent instance of anxiety or worry. Did you find it challenging to surrender those concerns to God in prayer? How did the act of presenting your requests to God affect your sense of anxiety or peace afterward?

2. Consider your approach to seeking guidance or clarity in difficult situations. Do you find it easier to rely on your own understanding or advice from others rather than presenting your requests to God in prayer? How might shifting this approach affect your sense of peace and trust in God's guidance?

CHAPTER TWENTY-EIGHT

DAY 28 - POWER SURGE FOR TODAY

FANNING THE FLAMES!

"Never lacking in zeal, but keep your spiritual fervor, serving the Lord."

Romans 12:11 NIV

Wouldn't it be nice if we never lost our zeal for something we are truly passionate about? Wouldn't it be nice if we never grew weary and had an endless supply of energy?

Maybe you have a big, audacious goal you are working on and you need to re-fuel your passion. This could be a passion for reclaiming your health, for building a new relationship, or even for creating a different life for yourself. Whatever your goal is, you definitely need zeal, great energy or enthusiasm to keep your pursuit or passion alive.

We are also told we should keep our spiritual fervor burning, to keep our zeal for serving the Lord alive. So often, we seem to grow weary and burn out, or we get overwhelmed with the busyness of life and our passion fades away.

Have you ever built a bonfire and then just watched it burn? When you started to build the fire, it was very small and it probably even needed some extra fuel or coaxing to catch fire. First you had to gather twigs, shrubs and debris that would help to get your fire burning quickly, and then once it was actually going you could begin to add bigger twigs and logs to the fire. Then finally you could sit and enjoy watching the flames grow to an impressive size, giving off an intense heat in very little time.

As you continued to add more fuel to the fire, the fire kept getting bigger and brighter. Once you decided to stop adding more fuel to the fire though, it stopped getting bigger. As the logs burned up and the flames died down, the intense heat and passion of the fire dwindled. The zeal of the fire diminished and after some time you were left with only the smoldering embers. Eventually, without continuing to nurture the fire, it all went out.

. . .

This is a great analogy of how we must remain fueled in our own passions and goals as well as in our spiritual fervor. Just like a bonfire burns brightly when fueled, so too we can burn brightly for Jesus when we are fueled and nourished in the Word. We are like a fire that needs constant fueling. When we first come to know the Lord, our flames may be small, but as we learn and grow, our lives can burn brightly like a bonfire.

If we want to keep our spiritual flame alive, it's essential to keep adding fuel to our fire. We must keep our zeal alive by intentionally staying in communion with God through prayer, reading the Word, listening to worship music, and by attending church and fellowshipping with other believers. These practices can quickly ignite the embers and strengthen our spiritual fervor, renewing our zeal for serving the Lord.

When we burn brightly and remain fueled in the word of God, we can inspire others to do the same. We become a beacon of light in a dark world, shining the love and grace of Christ to those around us. Let's serve the Lord with all our heart, and let our passion for Him ignite others to do the same.

Something to ponder:

. . .

1. Reflect on a time when your spiritual fervor felt particularly strong and vibrant. What practices or habits were you consistently engaging in during that period that fueled your passion for serving the Lord?

2. Think about moments when you've felt a decrease in spiritual zeal. What factors or distractions tend to diminish your fervor for God? How can you prioritize or rekindle those habits that fuel your spiritual passion?

CHAPTER TWENTY-NINE

DAY 29 - POWER SURGE FOR TODAY

MORNING SATISFACTION!

"Satisfy us in the morning with your unfailing love, that we may sing for joy and be glad all our days."
Psalm 90:14 NIV

Imagine waking up in the morning to the smell of freshly brewed coffee or to the aroma of a delicious breakfast being made specifically for you in the kitchen. I love coffee, so for me the feeling of satisfaction and contentment that comes from the aroma of a good cup of coffee makes me feel very content and satisfied. My heart sings for joy. If you don't care for coffee, the breakfast aroma might give you a similar feeling of contentment and satisfaction for the day.

. . .

The psalmist expresses this kind of satisfaction when he says, "Satisfy us in the morning with your unfailing love, that we may sing for joy and be glad all our days." This is a contentment that is far more valuable than a cup of coffee or a delicious breakfast, but the feeling of contentment and satisfaction is something we can relate to.

Just as we need food to nourish our bodies, our souls crave for the love and presence of God to satisfy our deepest needs. When we wake up each morning and seek the Lord's love, we can experience a sense of satisfaction and contentment that sustains us throughout the day. This deep satisfaction, this intense love from God in the morning can lead us to having our soul filled with joy, having a song in our heart, and having a contented spirit, regardless of our circumstances.

God's love is unfailing and always available to us, but we must intentionally seek it out each day. Just as we make time for breakfast or a cup of coffee in the morning, we must also make time for God and His love.

When we are satisfied with God's love, our hearts overflow with joy and gladness knowing that we are loved and cared for by our Heavenly Father. This then gives us the strength we need for each day to face whatever challenges come our way.

. . .

Praying you have this wonderful aroma today; praying that you have a satisfaction that lasts throughout your day basking in the Father's unfailing love for you.

Something to ponder:

1. Reflect on a time when you felt deeply satisfied and content in your spiritual life. What practices or habits contributed to that sense of fulfillment and closeness with God?

2. Consider your morning routines or habits. Do you prioritize seeking God's presence and love as part of your morning rituals? How might incorporating intentional moments with God at the start of your day impact your overall sense of satisfaction and joy?

CHAPTER THIRTY

DAY 30 - POWER SURGE FOR TODAY

FOUNDATION OF WISDOM!

"The fear of the Lord is the beginning of knowledge, but fools despise wisdom and instruction."
Proverbs 1:7 NIV

As we go through life, we encounter many challenges that require us to make decisions. Some decisions are easy to make, while others are more complex and require careful consideration and real wisdom. I would even say that some decisions require expert advice or wise counsel from others, and sometimes even legal advice.

A decision made today can really impact what our day will look like tomorrow. There are some definite consequences to our decisions. When we are facing decisions that are life altering, we need to do our due diligence and seek to understand, do the research and obtain the correct information and knowledge in order to make the right choice.

I immediately think of purchasing a house when I think about a life-altering decision. In my husband's career, he was transferred multiple times. This meant having to sell our current home in order to buy another house in the new city. Buying a home is a big purchase, and we always wanted the right knowledge and information about the house and about the location so that we could make a wise decision.

We would pray for wisdom and guidance and then we would do our own due diligence. We would talk to the realtor, call my father for advice, talk to the neighbors to find out more information about the area, and check to make sure the foundation of the house was solid. We wanted to be wise because we knew this one decision would impact our family's wellbeing for years to come.

In Proverbs 1:7, we read that the fear of the Lord is the beginning of knowledge. This means that if we want to have true knowledge and understanding, we must first have a healthy respect and awe for God. Just as a builder must lay a solid foundation before building a house, we must have a strong foundation of reverence for God before we can acquire true knowledge and wisdom.

So often though, in our hastiness with decision-making, we foolishly ignore the wisdom and instruction that comes from having a right relationship with God. We are like a builder who tries to build a house on the sand instead of on a solid foundation. We think we can do it on our own knowledge, but without God's wisdom and guidance, our lives will crumble and fall.

We need to seek God's knowledge and wisdom in every area of our lives. This may mean seeking outside help from a close friend or a pastor, or someone who is there to pray with you and to guide you to make the right decision.

Let's not be like fools who despise wisdom and instruction, but let's rather embrace the fear of the Lord as the beginning of knowledge, and trust in his guidance in every aspect of our lives. Just as a well-built house stands firm against the storms of life, so too will our lives be protected with the foundation of a strong relationship with God.

Something to ponder:

. . .

1. Reflect on a past decision where you sought guidance or wisdom from others. How did incorporating outside perspectives or seeking counsel impact the outcome of your decision?

2. Consider moments when you might have neglected seeking spiritual guidance or wisdom in decision-making. How might incorporating a reverence for God's guidance have influenced those situations differently?

www.ingramcontent.com/pod-product-compliance
Lightning Source LLC
Chambersburg PA
CBHW032041040426
42449CB00007B/976